RAINY DAY RHYMES

RAINY DAY RHYMES

SELECTED BY GAIL RADLEY

ILLUSTRATED BY ELLEN KANDOIAN

Houghton Mifflin Company
Boston   1992

Library of Congress Cataloging-in-Publication Data

Rainy day rhymes / selected by Gail Radley ; illustrated by Ellen
    Kandoian.
        p.   cm.
    Summary: A collection of poems about rainy days and nights, by
authors including Elizabeth Coatsworth, Myra Cohn Livingston, and
Aileen Fisher.
    ISBN 0-395-59967-9
    1. Rain and rainfall—Juvenile poetry.   2. Children's poetry,
American.   [1. Rain and rainfall—Poetry.   2. American poetry—
Collections.]   I. Radley, Gail.   II. Kandoian, Ellen, ill.
PS595.R33R35   1992   91-4244
811.008'036—dc20   CIP
                          AC

Printed in the United States of America
Copyright acknowledgments appear on page 47.

woz 10   9   8   7   6   5   4   3   2   1

With love to my daughter,
Jana, who helped.

—G.R.

With love to my sisters,
Janet and Nancy.

—E.K.

Contents

Rain

by Robert Louis Stevenson

The rain is raining all around,
    It falls on field and tree,
It rains on the umbrellas here,
    And on the ships at sea.

Spring Rain

by Marchette Chute

The storm came up so very quick
   It couldn't have been quicker.
I should have brought my hat along,
   I should have brought my slicker.

My hair is wet, my feet are wet,
   I couldn't be much wetter.
I fell into a river once
   But this is even better.

Rhyme

by Elizabeth Coatsworth

I like to see a thunder storm,
   A dunder storm,
     A blunder storm,
I like to see it, black and slow,
Come stumbling down the hills.

I like to hear a thunder storm,
   A plunder storm,
     A wonder storm,
Roar loudly at our little house
And shake the window sills!

Run in the Rain

by Aileen Fisher

I wore a newspaper raincoat,
I wore a newspaper hat,
and my feet
went spattering down the street
as fast as the rain could spat.

I must have looked rather funny,
but oh, the race was sport,
and when I dashed
to the door at last
I bet I dripped a quart.

Raining Again
by Dorothy Aldis

Raining again. And raining again.
Freckles of rain on the window pane.
It pricks into puddles like millions of pins.
For a minute it stops—
But then it begins.

And John flats his nose on the
Window pane
Watching and watching and
Watching the rain:
John can't remember
He's ever been
Any place else but
Always in!

Very Lovely

by Rose Fyleman

Wouldn't it be lovely if the rain came down
Till the water was quite high all over the town?
If the cabs and buses all were set afloat,
And we had to go to school in a little boat?

Wouldn't it be lovely if it still should pour
And we all went up to live on the second floor?
If we saw the butcher sailing up the hill,
And we took the letters in at the window sill?

It's been raining, raining, raining, all the afternoon;
All these things might happen really very soon.
If we woke to-morrow and found they had begun,
Wouldn't it be glorious? *Wouldn't* it be fun?

Others
by Harry Behn

Even though it's raining
I don't wish it wouldn't.
That would be like saying
I think that it shouldn't.
I'd rather be out playing
Than sitting hours and hours
Watching rain falling
In drips and drops and showers.
But what about the robins?
What about the flowers?

Raindrops

by Aileen Fisher

How brave a ladybug must be!
Each drop of rain is big as she.

Can you imagine what *you'd* do
if raindrops fell as big as you?

I Like It When It's Mizzly
by Aileen Fisher

I like it when it's mizzly
and just a little drizzly
so everything looks far away
and make-believe and frizzly.

I like it when it's foggy
and sounding very froggy.
I even like it when it rains
on streets and weepy window panes
and catkins on the poplar tree
and *me.*

Mud

by Polly Chase Boyden

Mud is very nice to feel
All squishy-squash between the toes!
I'd rather wade in wiggly mud
Than smell a yellow rose.

Nobody else but rosebush knows
How nice mud feels
Between the toes.

Umbrellas
by Rowena Bennett

When the rain is raining
 And April days are cool
All the big umbrellas
 Go bumping home from school.
They bump the blowing cloudburst,
 They push the pushing storm.
They leap a muddy puddle
Or get into a huddle
 To keep each other warm.

But who is underneath them
   You really cannot tell
Unless you know the overshoes
   Or rubbers very well
Or the flippy-flop galoshes
With their swishes and their swashes
Or the running rubber boots
With their scampers and their scoots . . .

Oh, when the rain is raining
   And April days are cool
I like to watch umbrellas
   Come bumping home from school!
I like to watch and wonder
Who's hiding halfway under . . .

City Rain

by Rachel Field

Rain in the city!
   I love to see it fall
Slantwise where buildings crowd
   Red brick and all.
Streets of shiny wetness
Where the taxis go,
With people and umbrellas all
   Bobbing to and fro.

Rain in the city!
   I love to hear it drip
When I am cozy in my room
   Snug as any ship,
With toys spread on the table,
   With a picture book or two,
And the rain like a rumbling tune that sings
Through everything I do.

Rainy Nights
by Irene Thompson

I like the town on rainy nights
　　When everything is wet—
When all the town has magic lights
　　And streets of shining jet!

When all the rain about the town
　　Is like a looking-glass,
And all the lights are upside down
　　Below me as I pass.

In all the pools are velvet skies,
　　And down the dazzling street
A fairy city gleams and lies
　　In beauty at my feet.

Storm Noises

by Rowena Bennett

The wind is mooing like a cow,
    The wind is stamping with its hoof,
The rain is pecking like a dove—
    Pick-pecking all along the roof.
The thunder gallops like a goat
    And tramples on a murky cloud;
And, though the sky is soft as mud,
    His footsteps echo long and loud.

Brooms
by Dorothy Aldis

On stormy days
When the wind is high
Tall trees are brooms
Sweeping the sky.

They swish their branches
In buckets of rain,
And swash and sweep it
Blue again.

Whether the Weather Be Fine

Anonymous

Whether the weather be fine,
Or whether the weather be not,
Whether the weather be cold,
Or whether the weather be hot,
We'll weather the weather
Whatever the weather
Whether we like it or not.

Understanding

by Myra Cohn Livingston

Sun
and rain
and wind
and storms
and thunder go together.

There has to be a little bit of each
to make the weather.

Index of Authors and Titles

Acknowledgments

Acknowledgment is made to the following publishers and authors or their representatives for their permission to use copyrighted material. Every reasonable effort has been made to clear the use of the poems in this volume with the copyright owners. If notified of any omissions, the editor and publisher will gladly make the proper corrections in future printings.

Dorothy Aldis for "Raining Again" and "Brooms," from *All Together,* published by Putnam, copyright © 1952 by Dorothy Aldis.

Doubleday for "City Rain," from *Taxis and Toadstools* by Rachel Field, copyright © 1926 by Doubleday, a division of Bantam Doubleday Dell Publishing Group, Inc. "Very Lovely," from *Fairies and Chimneys* by Rose Fyleman, copyright 1918, 1920 by George H. Doran. Used by permission of Doubleday, a division of Bantam Doubleday Dell Publishing Group, Inc.

HarperCollins Publishers for "Raindrops" by Aileen Fisher, from *Out from the Dark and Daylight,* copyright © 1980 by Aileen Fisher. "I Like It When It's Mizzly" by Aileen Fisher, from *I Like Weather,* copyright © 1963 by Aileen Fisher. "Run in the Rain" by Aileen Fisher, from *In One Door and Out the Other*, copyright © 1969 by Aileen Fisher. "Rainy Nights" by Irene Thompson, from *Come Follow Me,* published by Evans Bros./Unwin Hyman.

Killian Jordan for "Mud" by Polly Boyden.

Modern Curriculum Press, Inc. for "Storm Noises" by Rowena Bastin Bennett, from *The Day Is Dancing and Other Poems,* copyright © 1968 by Rowena Bastin Bennett. Reprinted by permission of Modern Curriculum Press, Inc.

Putnam Publishing Group for "Rhyme" by Elizabeth Coatsworth, reprinted by permission of Grosset & Dunlap, Inc. from *The Sparrow Bush,* copyright © 1966 by Grosset & Dunlap, Inc.

Marian Reiner for "Others" by Harry Behn, from *The Wizard in the Well,* copyright © 1956 by Harry Behn, copyright renewed 1984 by Alice Behn Goebel, Pamela Behn Adam, Peter Behn, and Prescott Behn. "Understanding" by Myra Cohn Livingston, from *The Moon and a Star and Other Poems*, copyright © 1965 by Myra Cohn Livingston. Reprinted by permission of Marian Reiner.

Mary Chute Smith for "Spring Rain" by Marchette Chute, from *Rhymes about the City*, copyright 1946 by Macmillan Publishing Company. Copyright renewed 1974 by E. P. Dutton. Permission to reprint granted by Mary Chase Smith.